Fifties Steam

Remembered

No. 61333 seen at Cambridge.

Fifties Steam
Remembered

ERIC SAWFORD

First published in the United Kingdom in 2003 by
Sutton Publishing Limited · Phoenix Mill
Thrupp · Stroud · Gloucestershire · GL5 2BU

British Library Cataloguing in Publication Data
A catalogue record for this book is available from the British Library

ISBN 0-7509-3154-X

Endpapers. Front: No. 41300 at Bricklayers Arms depot.
Back: No. 69001 approaching Hull Dairycoates.

Half-title page photograph: The 'Plant Centenarian' near Huntingdon.
Title page photograph: No. 41049 returning to Bedford.

Typeset in 10/12pt Palatino
Typesetting and origination by
Sutton Publishing Limited.
Printed and bound in England by
J.H. Haynes & Co. Ltd, Sparkford.

Contents

Jubilee class no. 45705 *Seahorse* was one of five members of the class allocated to Farnley Junction shed. In 1965 four still remained at the depot, among them no. 45562 *Alberta*, a great favourite on rail trips. Sadly it did not make it into preservation.

13.5.56

The seven members of the N15X class were rebuilds by Maunsell of London, Brighton & South Coast Railway L class 4–6–4Ts, introduced in 1914. Rebuilding commenced in 1934, and all were named. In the fifties the entire class was allocated to Basingstoke shed, with semi-fasts to London Waterloo being among their duties. No. 32328 *Hackworth* had just arrived at Nine Elms for servicing.

5.7.51

This was the only opportunity I had to photograph one of Drummond's L11 class – here is no. 30163 at its home shed, Nine Elms. Forty members of the class were built at the LSWR Nine Elms Works between 1904 and 1907. No. 30163, completed in September 1903, was among the last survivors, being withdrawn in October 1951. The class became extinct the following month.

5.7.51

Introduction

By the early fifties the railways had largely recovered from the problems resulting from the war years and the changes caused by nationalisation. Considerable amounts of track had been replaced, and much of the infrastructure had also received attention. Numerous speed restrictions had been lifted in turn, allowing expresses to run to timings similar to those in place before the war. Many older locomotives were still in active service, and some that had been withdrawn at the beginning of the war were given a second lease of life. But time was running out for these and other veterans as new engines were being constructed at an ever-increasing rate. The year 1951 saw the first of the Standard classes making their debut. Anyone who can recall this period will surely remember the interest caused by the Britannias. The first opportunity for enthusiasts to see no. 70004 *William Shakespeare* was at the Festival of Britain exhibition on the South Bank site in London. These grand locomotives were followed in due course by several other designs, some of them, in these austerity years, being little more than recent classes updated with Standard fittings. These were exciting times for all enthusiasts, and no one would have believed that within a few years steam would be finished in revenue-earning service.

The arrival of the steady stream of new locomotives soon resulted in numerous veterans making their last journey to oblivion. For the majority their passing received little attention other than a brief comment that a particular class had become extinct, and their entries in the society's list of withdrawn locomotives. There were, of course, a few exceptions. One was the last Great Northern Atlantic, no. 62822, which made its last journey over the route on which these grand engines had become famous, working the Ivatt 'Atlantic Special' to Doncaster.

Visits to many depots often revealed something of particular interest in the sidings, or tucked away at the side or in the back of a shed. It was an infuriating fact of life that photography was frequently impossible in such situations. Engines left outside were usually surrounded by coal dumps, wagons and general clutter, while inside the photographer had to contend with confined spaces and dark corners, making it impossible to obtain good pictures.

During most of the fifties numerous branches and cross-country lines were still active, and were often worked by veterans reaching the end of their days. All this was to change with the commencement of the Beeching cuts. The subsequent line closures included a number of cross-country routes; these were not high revenue earners but they did make connections much easier. Several decades later hindsight shows that the retention of such lines would have made an important contribution to handling freight, if not passenger services. One that disappeared was the Cambridge–Bletchley line which gave access to the East Coast, Midland and West Coast main lines as well as handling a large amount of goods traffic – to the extent that a flyover was built at Bletchley to facilitate through-routed freight. Only the section between Bedford and Bletchley was not closed, and currently there are plans to reinstate an east–west link, using the existing Cambridge to Hitchin line, the East Coast main line to Sandy and then a new section constructed to link up at Bedford.

Several other cross-country routes in the east of the country also disappeared, notably the Cambridge–Kettering, Peterborough–Rugby, Peterborough–Northampton and, to a lesser degree, Hitchin–Bedford lines.

M7 class locomotives were a familiar sight throughout the fifties working empty stock in and out of Waterloo. No. 30123 was one of a number of examples of the class allocated to Nine Elms. Built in 1903, it remained in service until July 1959, and the class became extinct in 1964. Alongside is King Arthur class no. 30457 *Sir Bedivere*.

5.7.51

The rail map in the early and mid-fifties changed dramatically in the later years of the decade and by 1959 it was very different indeed. Many lines had already gone, or were about to be closed, leaving numerous towns without a rail service. Numerous holiday resorts like Hunstanton in Norfolk, which at one time attracted considerable excursion traffic, lost their rail links. This led to the increasing use of private cars and coaches, which further reduced the demand for efficient rail services.

Some of the lines marked for closure attracted rail tours, although not all these routes had been used by passenger services. Enthusiasts' specials were often to be seen making a journey over a particular line shortly before closure. Somersham to Ramsey East had lost its passenger service on 22 September 1930, although it remained open for a weekdays-only daily goods train. There were occasional passenger trains too, especially during the summer when a few excursions ran to the coast and there were also specials to Yarmouth races. Before closure it hosted several enthusiasts' specials. The entire line was not closed, as the section between Somersham and Warboys remained in use for traffic to and from the brickworks until July 1964.

Such was the interest in the vanishing branch lines that even those unable to accept passenger stock were not missed out by the enthusiasts' specials, determined to travel the route for one last time. The Benwick branch was purely goods, serving agricultural businesses and farmers. This did not stop several hundred enthusiasts travelling over the line in open wagons headed by a J17 class 0–6–0 – no one minded clambering into the rather dirty rolling stock, or being subjected to smuts and drifting smoke on the journey. Sadly, the majority of these lines disappeared completely, leaving no trace of their existence.

The variety of motive power to be seen during the fifties was extraordinary, and it was not uncommon to see locomotives that had completed seventy years' service or more. The three Beattie 2–4–0Ts working the Wenford Bridge mineral line in Cornwall attracted

2

countless enthusiasts. This class was originally built to handle suburban traffic, and the three survivors outlived their contemporaries by a great many years, the last of their former classmates having been withdrawn in 1898. Over the years the three survivors had been considerably rebuilt, and all had received Drummond boilers. All three survived the decade, and fortunately one has made it into preservation.

The Southern Region had a range of interesting small tank locomotives still in action in the fifties. Those fortunate enough to enjoy a holiday on the south coast, especially enthusiasts visiting the Lyme Regis branch, will surely remember the three elegant 0415 class 4–4–2Ts that worked the service here. These were the last survivors of a class of seventy-one engines designed by W. Adams for the London & South Western Railway and constructed in 1882–5 by four private companies. By 1928 only two remained in service with the Southern Railway, the remainder having been withdrawn or sold. The two survivors were retained for the Lyme Regis branch. In 1946 the Southern decided that a third locomotive was necessary to allow for maintenance and overhaul. Luckily another 4–4–2T was available, albeit in a rather sorry state. It had been sold to the government way back in 1917 and later passed to the East Kent Railway, from which it was purchased for £800. All three locomotives were withdrawn in 1961 after a long association with the Lyme Regis branch, and were replaced by Ivatt 2–6–2Ts. Adams no. 30583 (488), the only survivor of the trio, was rescued for preservation by the Bluebell Railway.

Royal Scot class no. 41623 *Royal Irish Fusilier* heading 'The Manxman' takes water at Rugby. This engine was allocated to 8A Edge Hill depot. It was photographed before smoke deflectors were fitted to the rebuilt locomotives.

3.7.51

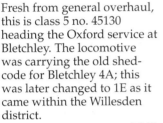

In the early fifties Cambridge shed had three Ivatt 2MT 2–6–0s, whose duties were normally on the Colne Valley line. This is no. 46465, photographed at Godmanchester heading the Kettering–Cambridge service. This was unusual as the single out and return working from Cambridge to Kettering was in the hands of J15 0–6–0s until the line closed in 1959.

18.9.51

Fresh from general overhaul, this is class 5 no. 45130 heading the Oxford service at Bletchley. The locomotive was carrying the old shed-code for Bletchley 4A; this was later changed to 1E as it came within the Willesden district.

6.8.51

Nottingham Victoria with A5s nos 69806 and 69825 awaiting departure. Locomotives of this class were allocated to Colwick and Grantham depots and worked services to Derby and Grantham. Both the locomotives pictured were built at Gorton Works in 1911 and 1923 respectively, and were classified A5/1. The thirteen post-Grouping engines built by Hawthorn Leslie in 1925/6 became class A5/2.

6.7.51

Further along the coast two diminutive class C14 0–4–0Ts could be found shunting on Southampton Quay. These also had a very interesting history. They were originally constructed for rail-motor work to the design of D. Drummond as 2–2–0Ts. In all ten were built, seven of which were sold to the government during the First World War and never returned. The three survivors were converted into 0–4–0Ts. One was later transferred to departmental stock as no. 77s and was employed at Redbridge sleeper depot. The last in service was withdrawn in 1959. Sadly none has survived.

At the other end of the scale a visit to Feltham depot had much to offer, with a number of large tank locomotives in its allocation, including the massive G16 4–8–0Ts built for hump shunting work in Feltham marshalling yard and the class H16 4–6–2Ts designed for short distance freight workings. Both classes were designed by R.W. Urie for the London & South Western Railway and were introduced in 1921.

By comparison the locomotive stock of the Western Region consisted of more Standard designs. Only South Wales boasted more variety, and enthusiasts could find here numerous types of tank locomotive originally owned by a variety of Welsh railways and later absorbed into the Great Western. Sadly, the writing was already on the wall for many of these engines, and as the fifties progressed the number of designs rapidly diminished.

The Great Western also made considerable use of 0–4–2Ts for rail-motor work on branches and cross-country services. These locomotives, designed by C.B. Collett and built in 1932–6, had tall chimneys that made them look older than they actually were. Withdrawals commenced in 1956, but forty survived into the sixties.

There is only space in this introduction to mention a few examples from the fascinating range of motive power at work in the fifties. For me personally one of the highlights was the famous 'Lickey Banker' on the London Midland Region. This massive 0–10–0 no. 58100 was designed by W. Fowler and built by the Midland Railway in 1919. After a life spent blasting its way up the Lickey incline it was withdrawn in 1956. Unfortunately it was scrapped; it would have been an ideal engine for preservation as part of the National Collection.

In 1923 the former London & North Western Railway was one of the principal companies that merged to form the LMS. By the start of the fifties none of its passenger locomotives was still in service. The remaining ex-LNWR locomotive stock consisted largely of 0–8–0s. These were almost identical engines, although some had been built as 2–8–0s. Well liked and powerful, these engines will be widely remembered for their sharp exhaust note and asthmatic sounds. During the early fifties only a small number of other ex-LNWR locomotives were still in service. These comprised a few 0–6–0s of two designs known as 'Cauliflowers' and 'Coal Engines'. Several of the latter ended their days at Crewe Works on shunting duties. The tank version, referred to simply as 'Coal Tanks', were 0–6–2Ts. Most of this class, once three hundred strong and introduced by F.W. Webb in 1881, remained unaltered throughout their long working lives. They were also noted for their sharp exhaust note. The majority of those that came into British Railways stock were withdrawn by 1955. One exception was no. 58926 which carried on until 1958, and happily this grand old lady has survived into preservation.

The Midland Railway had followed a small engine policy, as a result of which considerable numbers of 4–4–0s passed into BR stock. Some were constructed before the Grouping in 1923, others were built in LMS days to basically similar designs. Engines with this wheel arrangement worked on both main and secondary lines. Bedford depot had a sizeable batch of Compounds which worked the St Pancras local and semi-fast services until they were replaced by Standard class 4 engines of tank and tender designs.

In the Eastern Region the principal main line expresses were in the hands of Pacifics, with the workhorse V2 class 2–6–2s often used as standby engines. One exception was the single W1 class 4–6–4, no. 10000, originally built by the LNER in 1929 as a 4-cylinder compound with a water-tube boiler. In 1937 it was rebuilt as a 3-cylinder conventional locomotive. It was a familiar sight for most of the fifties until it was scrapped in 1959.

Looking rather out of place deep in London Midland Region territory, 5100 class no. 5139 awaits departure from Crewe station with a train for Wellington.

3.7.51

The E4 class 2–4–0s at Cambridge attracted much interest as they were the last 2–4–0 tender engines in service. At Cambridge they were restricted to local branches, the Colne Valley line and pilot duties. However, it was not unknown for an E4 to deputise on the first train of the day to Kettering and on the return working in the late afternoon. This was normally a J15 0–6–0 duty. The last survivor was no. 62785, a long-time Cambridge engine. Luckily it is still with us, magnificently restored to its Great Eastern blue livery.

In the north-east it was the 0–8–0s of the Q6 class that I remember best. These 2-cylinder locomotives were powerful and well liked by enginemen. The Q7s were a numerically much smaller class, and these 3-cylinder engines were often to be seen on Consett–Tyne Dock workings. The North Eastern Railway also had a class of fifteen 4–8–0Ts, first introduced by W. Worsdell in 1909 for heavy shunting work. By the mid-fifties work for them was getting scarce, and three were to be found stored at Newport.

I personally found the railways north of the border very interesting, with numerous pre-Grouping designs from the North British, Caledonian and Great North of Scotland Railways still to be found hard at work there in the early years of the fifties. In addition there were two Highland Railway 0–4–4Ts working the Dornoch branch. These were replaced in 1957 by – of all things – GWR 0–6–0 Pannier tanks.

There were numerous 4–4–0s to be found working local and secondary services in Scotland. Those of North British origin included some that were very unfamiliar to visitors from the south. Tank locomotives included sturdy class Y9 0–4–0STs with their rather decrepit-looking wooden tenders, as well as the Caledonian version referred to simply as 'Pugs'. The docks in Aberdeen were the usual working place for four ex-Great North of Scotland Railway 0–4–2Ts of class Z4 and Z5. The main difference between them was that the two Z4s had 3ft 6in diameter wheels while those of the Z5s were larger at 4ft. These locomotives were built for use at the harbour in 1915.

These are just a few random insights into what was around in the fifties. Many classes and sole survivors that were taken over in 1948 did not even last until 1950, and for those that did their days were numbered. The arrival of new engines released many for lesser duties, and the knock-on effect of this brought about the end for countless veterans. Towards the end of the decade line closures and the introduction of increasing numbers of diesel locomotives and railcars resulted in further inroads being made into the steam locomotive stock. By the dawn of the sixties Britain's railways were very different, and in 1968 all steam in normal revenue-earning service finished. In some parts of the country this move had already taken place. Unquestionably the fifties were a milestone in our railway history and the pictures in this book have been carefully chosen to illustrate the fascinating range of motive power to be seen at that time.

For me it has certainly been a trip down memory lane. I find it hard to believe that it was really all those years ago. We are fortunate that a considerable number of locomotives have survived into preservation and many have been fully restored to working order. They are a fitting tribute to the British engineering skills that built and maintained these great engines.

Eric Sawford
Huntingdon, August 2002

Although it was a March engine, I only had one opportunity to photograph Sandringham class no. 61633 *Hinchingbrooke*. The engine is pictured at St Ives heading a Cambridge to King's Lynn train.

14.7.51

During the very early fifties visitors to Yarmouth Beach shed on a Sunday would be sure of finding several F6 2–4–2Ts present as five were allocated to the depot. No. 67235, seen here, still carries British Railways markings on its tank sides. The Yarmouth F6s were used on Lowestoft and Potter Higham services. No. 67235 was built in 1911 and withdrawn in January 1956.

12.8.51

The British Railways Regions

There were six regions in the fifties, and all depots had a specific shed-code. Those on the London Midland Region were allocated from 1A Willesden to 28B Fleetwood. Next came the Eastern, ranging from 30A Stratford, one of the largest depots with well over four hundred engines in its allocation, to the much smaller 40F Boston. The North Eastern commenced with York 50A and ran to 54D Consett. The system then went north of the border, with 60A Inverness to 68E Carlisle Canal. This left two regions, the Southern, with 70A Nine Elms London to 75G Eastbourne, and the Western, starting with 81A Old Oak Common and extending to 89C Machynlleth in central Wales. During the fifties numerous changes of shed-codes took place, some of them being inter-regional. The codes used herein refer to the situation in the early fifties.

Visiting some depots you would find a mixture of locomotives types, 9E Trafford Park for example had both ex-LMS and ex-LNER engines. In addition some depots regularly serviced visitors from other regions. A typical example was Bletchley, where a D16 Claud Hamilton class 4–4–0 from Cambridge was often to be found, attracting much interest from enthusiasts travelling on the West Coast main line. Eastern Region engines were often to be found at Hither Green, having worked through with inter-regional freights.

The Western Region

The Great Western Railway had its own standardisation policy in force for many years and as a result the locomotive fleet consisted of a number of principal classes when the GWR was absorbed into the Western Region in 1948. A few examples of earlier designs were still in service, including the Saints and the Stars. The main passenger engines were the King class 4–6–0s and the Castles, with new locomotives still under construction at this time. The maids of all work were the Halls. The heavy freight engines of the Great Western were the sturdy 2800 class 2–8–0s. Initially a few of the ROD class 2–8–0s were also still active. Despite having been fitted with typical GWR equipment the outline of a Robinson Great Central engine was still easily distinguishable. There was a further small class of 2–8–0s in the shape of the 4700s, just nine in number. These were used on fast goods, but during the summer months it was far from unknown for them to work excursions and specials. One feature of the Western Region was the large number of 0–6–0 Pannier tanks. The 5700 class was the most numerous with 863 examples. Taken together with several other classes, the total figure was well over a thousand.

Each region had its followers but the Western was certainly highly rated, not just among enthusiasts living within the region's boundaries but also by many others from different parts of the country.

The first of the taper boiler 9400 class made its debut in 1947, to the design of Hawksworth for the Great Western Railway. Many were built by private contractors, the last being delivered in 1956, giving them the distinction of being the last pre-nationalisation designed locomotives to be built. No. 9426 is seen at Banbury.

27.3.55

Sparkling in the autumn sunshine Castle class no. 5094 *Tretower Castle* runs into Paddington. Castles were a familiar sight at the head of many express trains. These powerful and well-liked engines were developed from the 4–6–0 Stars and were introduced by Collett in 1923. Several were rebuilds, but the vast majority were of new construction.

9.9.59

Castle class no. 7030 *Cranbrook Castle* takes water at Cardiff General while heading a Swansea to Paddington express.

30.8.55

There was a continual stream of engine movements at busy times on Plymouth Laira depot. Castle class no. 4037 *The South Wales Borderers* is seen here leaving the shed. The locomotive had been on Old Oak Common's allocation before moving to the West Country. Note the regimental crest carried below the nameplate. This was one of the class members converted from a Star class 4–6–0.

5.9.56

Castle class no. 5033 *Broughton Castle* leaves Paddington for servicing. One of the station pilots has already taken the stock out. No. 5033 was a Chester engine at the time this picture was taken.

9.9.59

Castle class no. 5071 *Spitfire* was a Newton Abbot engine, and it is seen here having worked 'The Cornishman' to Bristol. One of the depot's maintenance staff takes the opportunity to wipe the ash from his face. Cleaning out the fireboxes of locomotives was an unpleasant job at the best of times, but especially in hot weather.

31.8.55

Out to grass! Castle class no. 4086 *Builth Castle*, a Plymouth Laira engine, had presumably failed near Reading and was dumped on an isolated siding near the shed. Note the huge lumps of coal on the tender, not a welcome sight for the fireman.

7.8.55

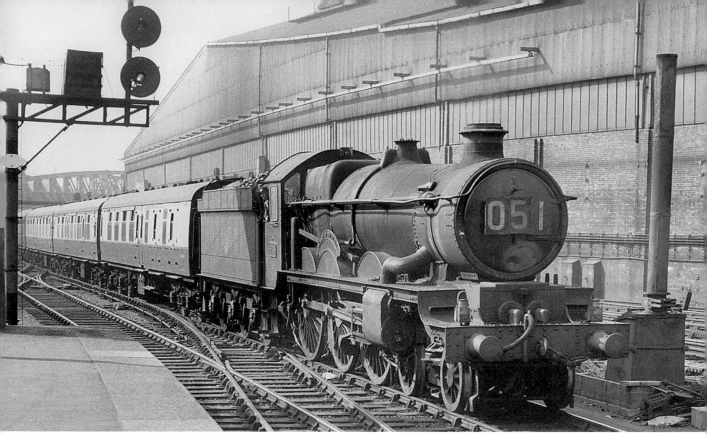

Signs of hard running are evident on the smokebox door of Castle class no. 5045 *Earl of Dudley*, seen here arriving at Paddington with a train from Worcester. The locomotive would wait at the buffers until one of Paddington's station pilots took the stock out, releasing the locomotive to run on for servicing.

9.9.59

The relief locomotive crew slowly walk up the platform at Bristol Temple Meads as Hall class no. 4962 *Ragley Hall* runs in. The train is carrying reporting number 585. On the left of the picture is one of the legions of pannier tanks that were to be seen throughout the region.

30.8.55

The pioneer member of the Hall class was no. 4900 *Saint Martin*, a rebuild by Collett of the Saint class with 6ft driving wheels. This was a forerunner of a numerous class used on everything from express duties to goods. No. 4900, photographed at Newton Abbot, was a Laira engine, having moved to the West Country from Worcester.

4.9.56

Hall class no. 5992 *Horton Hall* from Taunton shed stands in company with no. 7020 *Gloucester Castle* from Cardiff Canton at Bristol Bath Road, awaiting their return workings. Note the piles of ash and clinker lying around, a familiar sight at numerous depots.

31.8.55

In the mid-fifties Banbury was a sizeable depot with an allocation of sixty-five locomotives, mostly goods and shunting engines. In addition twelve Hall class 4–6–0s were to be found there. No. 4933 *Himley Hall* was a visitor from Oxford, the district's principal shed.

24.11.54

The 4900 class Halls were the class 5 mixed traffic locomotives of the Western Region, with 258 in service, excluding the later Modified Halls of 6959 class. These engines were to be found on most of the Western Region with the exception of parts of central Wales. The Halls had a powerful tractive effort of 27,275lb, compared with the 25,455lb of the LMR class 5 and 26,880lb of the Eastern Region B1s. All operated at a boiler pressure of 225lb. No. 4938 *Liddington Hall* is seen here at Oxford.

31.10.54

Grange class no. 6837 *Northampton Grange* on the through road at Cardiff General station while on station pilot duty, under the watchful eye of a young enthusiast.

30.8.55

Grange class no. 6804 *Brocklington Grange* takes water at Bristol Temple Meads. The driver has returned to the footplate, and refilling the tender has begun under the supervision of the fireman. In order to save time, two youthful locomotive men move coal forward on the tender.

30.8.55

The Grange class consisted of eighty locomotives. They were a variation of the Halls with smaller wheels and incorporating certain parts of withdrawn Moguls. Principally designed for parcels and fast goods, they were frequently to be seen on passenger duties. Here, no. 6824 *Ashley Grange* stands at Truro with a train for Penzance.

4.9.56

Worcester depot must have been short of engines as Grange class no. 6877 *Llanfair Grange* has been pressed into service to work a Paddington express instead of the usual Castle or Hall. Here no. 6877, released from its train, goes off for servicing before working home. Granges had a similar power classification to the Halls but had smaller driving wheels.

7.5.55

Engines from South Wales depots were not uncommon at Oxford. Grange class no. 6844 *Penhydd Grange*, a Llanelly engine, has just arrived on shed and is receiving attention from depot staff. Cleaning the firebox was a heavy, dirty job. Note the piles of ash at the side and the wagons standing alongside, already partly loaded.

24.11.54

Here, 2800 class no. 3817 rumbles along on the through road at Cardiff General with a heavy mixed goods as youthful enthusiasts race along the platform. The locomotive is carrying a disc lettered H2 on the right-hand lamp iron. In the background Hall class no. 4968 *Shotton Hall* awaits departure time.

30.8.55

At many depots during the early fifties even goods locomotives received the attention of cleaners: 2800 class no. 3841 seen here at Bristol St Phillips Marsh had recently been cleaned. This was a Collett locomotive, introduced in 1938. They had side-window cabs and other detail alterations to the Churchward engines introduced in 1903.

31.8.55

Here, 2800 class no. 3855 stands at Reading depot ready to work back to its home shed in South Wales. Engines of this type worked heavy coal trains from the South Wales collieries. Their route took them through the notorious Severn Tunnel where enginemen often used respirators owing to the time the freights took to travel through.

7.8.55

Weak late autumn sunshine picks out the details on 2800 class no. 2847 at Oxford. Churchward introduced these Great Western workhorses in 1903. In the early fifties 167 were still in service, including those introduced by Collett in 1938 that had detail alterations and side-window cabs.

31.10.54

The depot at Swansea Victoria was of London & North Western Railway origin.
It became part of the Western Region in 1949 and received the shed-code 87K. In
the early fifties the locomotives to be found there were all of LMS and LNWR
designs. Later in the decade a considerable number of ex-Great Western engines
were transferred to the shed. Here three former LMS locomotives await their
next duty: 8F 2–8–0 no. 48328, 3F 0–6–0T no. 47478 and 4MT 2–6–4T no. 42388.

31.8.55

ROD class no. 3023 on the turntable at Reading, having recently been transferred to Tyseley from Pontypool Road. The unmistakable outline of a Robinson 2–8–0 can be clearly seen despite the Great Western fittings. These engines, classified ROD class, were purchased from the Railway Operating Division of the Royal Engineers after the First World War in 1919.

7.8.55

ROD class no. 3012 was a Pontypool Road engine. It had obviously run into trouble on its journey from South Wales and was awaiting repair at Oxford with 'not to be moved' signs on both sides of the buffer beam.

31.10.54

The Great Western moguls were mixed traffic engines classified 4MT. With 5ft 8in driving wheels they were capable of a fair turn of speed. Locomotives of this type were often seen on specials during the fifties. No. 6331 was a Chester engine, pictured here on Reading shed.

7.8.55

The famous Great Western moguls, designed by Churchward, were first introduced in 1911 with subsequent batches built in later years, the last with side-window cabs and other detail alterations. No. 4375, seen here on a winter's day at Oxford, was one of the original batch. The majority of the 43XX series had already been withdrawn when this picture was taken.

27.2.55

Recently ex-works, 2251 class 0–6–0 no. 2211 takes water at Exeter depot. Only one member of this class was allocated to the depot which had thirty-two locomotives on its books. These included eight 0–4–2Ts and twelve Pannier tanks. Passenger locomotives were represented by two Castles and two Halls.

4.9.56

There was only one class of locomotives with an 0–6–0 wheel arrangement on the Western Region in the mid fifties – the 2251 class totalling 120 examples. The once-numerous Dean goods had all been withdrawn. No. 2289 was a visitor at Oxford, and only one member of the class was allocated to that depot. Although the engine is very grimy the letter G from Great Western can be clearly seen on the tender.

27.2.55

The coaling plant at St Phillips Marsh in Bristol was continuously in use feeding the depot's allocation of over 140 locomotives. Here 2251 class 0–6–0 no. 2201 and an 8F 2–8–0 are receiving supplies. Note the large water tank that was situated above the coaling positions. Eight members of the 2251 class were based at this depot in the mid-fifties.

31.8.55

The 9000 class, with their tall chimneys, huge domes and outside frames, always looked older than they actually were. Introduced in 1936 by Collett, they were a combination of Duke-type boilers and Bulldog frames and inevitably they soon acquired the nickname 'Dukedogs'. They were intended for use on secondary lines and several were employed in central Wales. One of the exceptions was no. 9015, an Oxford engine, seen here being shunted on a cold winter's day.

27.2.55

Several of the large 2–8–2Ts of class 7200 were usually to be seen at Oxford. The depot had four in its allocation, including no. 7238 seen here. The fifty-four members of the class were rebuilds of the 52XX design with an extended bunker and trailing wheels. These powerful engines were used on mineral workings.

31.10.54

The sturdy members of the 5200 class 2–8–0Ts were extensively used in South Wales on coal traffic, together with the Collett 2–8–2T rebuilds of the class listed in the 72XX series. Here no. 5264 of Newport Ebbw Junction prepares to take water at Bristol before working home through the notorious Severn Tunnel with a long train of coal empties.

31.8.55

Six members of the 6100 class 2–6–2Ts were allocated to Oxford. No. 6138, seen here, was among them. The majority of these engines were to be found in the London area with Old Oak Common, Slough, Southall and Reading all having sizeable numbers allocated. The class was introduced in 1931 principally for London suburban work.

27.2.55

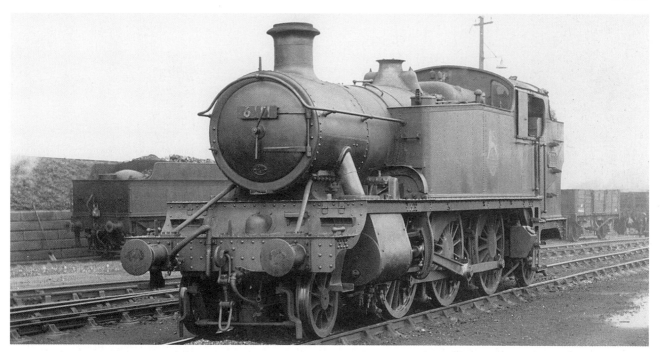

The 61XX class was introduced by Collett in 1931. A development of earlier locomotives with increased boiler pressure, they were intended for working in the London suburban area. In the fifties the majority were to be found there, working in and out of Paddington on passenger and empty stock duties. No. 6111, photographed at its home depot Oxford, was one of the exceptions.

31.10.54

Here 6100 class no. 6146 runs into Paddington to take out empty stock. Fourteen of these locomotives were allocated to Old Oak Common in 1954, principally for suburban workings, with others at Slough, Southall and Reading. No. 6146 was a Slough engine.

9.9.59

The locomotives of the 4500 class allocated to the Bristol area were employed on a wide variety of work ranging from local passenger duties to station pilots. No. 5561 was just one of twenty-three allocated to Bristol Bath Road shed. This depot was principally the home of engines used on passenger work while St Phillips Marsh was concerned with freight and shunting engines.

31.8.55

The 9400 class taper boiler 0–6–0PTs were designed for heavy shunting work and were introduced by Hawksworth for the Great Western. A considerable number were built well into BR days. No. 8405 was one of nine members of the class allocated to Banbury shed.

27.3.55

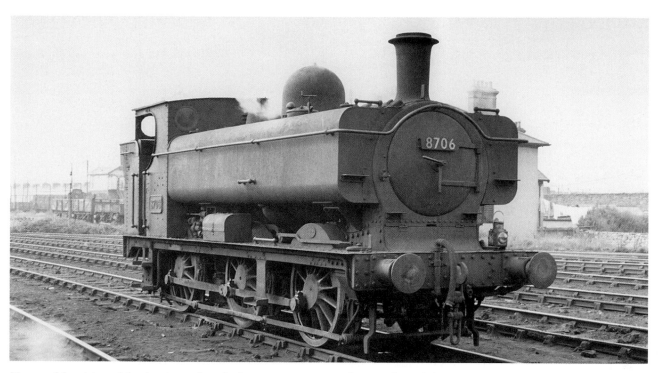

You could not travel far in steam days before you encountered a member of the 5700 class Pannier tanks, which was hardly surprising given that 863 were in service in the early fifties. No. 8706 was a typical example, photographed at its home shed Swansea (Paxton Street).

30.8.55

This is 5600 class no. 5655, a Merthyr engine, under repair at Cardiff East Dock. The middle set of driving wheels has been removed and the engine lacks its front numberplate and shed-code. In the background is one of the depot's many Pannier tanks. Cardiff East Dock, shed-code 88B, had seventy locomotives allocated to it in the mid-fifties, among them several 0–6–2Ts of Rhymney & Taff Vale Railway origin.

30.8.55

At larger depots there was an almost constant movement of locomotives to get the engines into position for their next working or for repairs and maintenance. Here Pannier no. 9654 is being moved by a Hall class engine at Oxford. These Panniers were classified as the 5700 class and were first introduced in 1929. There was considerable variation among the 863 examples, and some were equipped with condensing gear for working over the Metropolitan line.

31.10.54

The 5600 class was extensively used in South Wales. At the time of my visit to Cardiff East Dock shed there were at least three in the yard in various stages of repair. No. 5617 is seen here minus its coupling rods and trailing wheels. The locomotive at this time was allocated to Abercynon depot, also within the Cardiff district.

30.8.55

Poised to leave Cardiff East Dock depot is ex-Rhymney Railway 0–6–2T no. 36, carrying a disc headcode marked D7. This class was introduced in 1921 by Hurry Riches as class R1, a development of the much earlier R design. In the background is one of the ex-Taff Vale 0–6–2Ts allocated to this shed.

30.8.55

The 1361 class 0–6–0STs were introduced by Churchward in 1910 and designed for dock shunting. Four of the five built were allocated to Laira in the mid-fifties, the fifth being at Taunton. No. 1361, seen here about to replenish its water supply, was the first built. This picture includes a once very familiar water crane and heating stove intended to prevent winter freeze-ups.

5.9.56

The unmistakable outline of a Peckett design is readily apparent in this picture of 0–4–0ST no. 1152 at Swansea East Dock. Built in 1907, these locomotives were originally intended for Powlesland & Mason contractors, later passing into Great Western ownership. Note the warning bell in front of the cab and plate 26 duty number.
30.8.55

Reading had three of these 1400 class 0–4–2Ts in its allocation, but no. 1442 was an Oxford engine. These nippy little locomotives were usually employed on push-pull workings on branch and secondary lines throughout the Western Region.

7.8.55

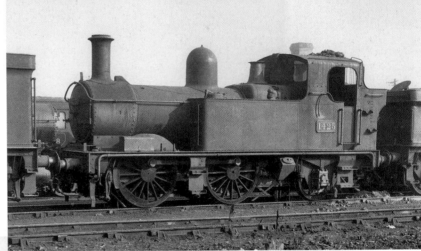

The 1400 class 0–4–2Ts, with their tall chimneys and large domes, also looked older than they were. Collett introduced the class for push-pull working on branch and secondary lines in 1932. No. 1425 was an Oxford engine for many years. These locomotives had 5ft 2in driving wheels and were capable of a fair turn of speed.

27.2.55

The following year, 1933, Collett's 5800 class made their debut. Unlike the 1400 class, they were not fitted with push-pull equipment, although otherwise the two types were identical. No. 5803 is seen here at its home depot Oxford, which in the mid-fifties had three 1400 and two 5800 class locomotives in its allocation.

27.2.55

The last narrow gauge locomotives in normal revenue service to be owned by British Railways were the three 2–6–2Ts working the Vale of Rheidol line. No. 8 *Llywelyn* was photographed at Devils Bridge ready for its return journey to Aberystwyth. The locomotive was in fully lined green livery, but this was later changed to plain blue.

15.7.59

This picture shows *Llywelyn*'s rather cramped cab conditions. This engine was built at Swindon in 1923 together with no. 7 *Owain Glyndwr*. The third engine, no. 9 *Prince of Wales*, was built by Davies Metcalfe in 1902 and rebuilt at Swindon in 1923.

15.7.59

The streamlined Western Region diesel railcars were allocated to steam depots. No. W15W, seen here at Oxford, was built in 1936 and was fitted with two engines giving 242bhp. It was fitted with seventy seats. There were thirty-eight railcars with considerable variation in size, two of which were built to handle parcel traffic.

31.10.54

The Southern Region

Although it did not have as many steam locomotives as other regions, the Southern could boast a considerable number of very interesting small tank engines. One outpost was at Wadebridge in Cornwall where the three Beattie 2–4–0 well tanks worked the Wenford branch. This was to become a mecca for enthusiasts and the Beatties surely became some of the most photographed steam engines in British Railways service. Also in the West Country the Adams 4–4–2Ts on the Lyme Regis branch attracted much attention. Perhaps less well known was the shunting work carried out on Southampton Town Quay by the diminutive C14 class 0–4–0Ts.

For many the main attraction on the Southern were the Bulleid Pacifics. The streamlined Merchant Navy class made their appearance in 1941, a time of severe austerity. In due course the entire class was rebuilt. The lightweight Pacifics were introduced in 1945, the first examples being known as the West Country class, with the Battle of Britain class arriving in the following year. These were also streamlined, and again many were later rebuilt.

Bournemouth depot's Lord Nelson class no. 30863 *Lord Rodney* stands ready at Nine Elms for its return working. Maunsell introduced this class of sixteen to the Southern Railway in 1926. Modifications carried out by Bulleid included the fitting of multiple jet blast pipes and a large chimney.

5.7.51

Ash, clinker, coal and water could usually be found around the pits at numerous depots and Bricklayers Arms depot was no exception. Battle of Britain class no. 34080 *74 Squadron*, a visitor, was in the process of receiving attention prior to working back to its home depot.

25.11.54

King Arthur class no. 30789 *Sir Guy* in Eastleigh shed with its valve gear dismantled. In the background is Schools class no. 30904 *Lancing*, fresh from works overhaul. Eastleigh was a modern fifteen-road shed, and several King Arthurs were allocated there in the fifties.

8.11.55

The graceful T9 class 4–4–0s introduced by the London & South Western Railway in 1899 were nicknamed 'Greyhounds'. By the fifties their days on express duties had long finished but they were still to be seen on specials and cross-country routes and also on lines such as the Padstow branch in Cornwall. No. 30705, a Basingstoke engine, is seen here at Nine Elms.

12.7.54

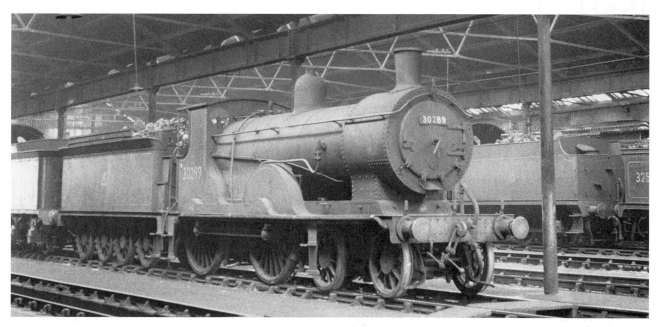

Eastleigh shed was reasonably airy and light, so photographs could just about be taken without a tripod. T9 no. 30289 was one of those allocated to the depot. Among their duties were local passenger and parcel trains. This engine was built at Nine Elms Works and completed in November 1899. Dubs & Company built other members of the class. No. 30283 was withdrawn in December 1957.

8.11.55

The graceful D class 4–4–0s, introduced by Wainwright in 1901 were principal express locomotives in their heyday but by the fifties the survivors had been relegated to secondary duties. No. 31549, photographed at Ashford, was engaged on shunting. Built in 1906 at Ashford Works it completed fifty years' service.

1.7.53

D15 class no. 30465, the last survivor, stands at Eastleigh. Time had nearly run out for this engine as it was withdrawn in June 1956. During its forty-four years in service it ran well over one-and-a-half million miles.

8.11.55

In 1955 only two of the ten D15 class 4–4–0s designed by Drummond for the London & South Western Railway still remained in service. All were built in 1912 at Eastleigh Works. They were powerful, free-running locomotives, well liked by enginemen, and were employed on express services. The last two members of the class were allocated to Nine Elms. In their final years they were still working on passenger turns or parcels and empty stock. No. 30467 was withdrawn in September 1955.

12.7.54

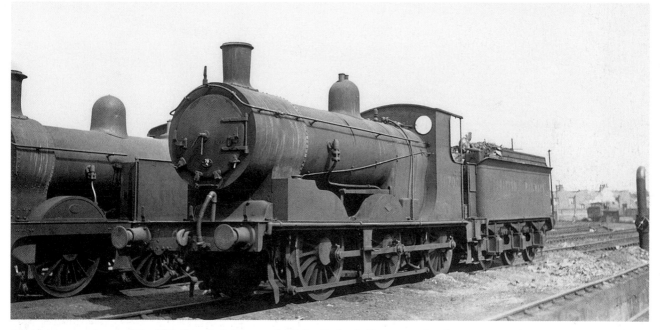

The thirty members of the 700 class 0–6–0s were built by Dubs & Company for the London & South Western Railway. Seen here at its home shed Nine Elms no. 30700 was completed in May 1897. All thirty survived to be taken into Southern stock at Grouping and the class was still intact at nationalisation. Withdrawals commenced in 1957 as a result of an accident, but it was another two years before any more were withdrawn. Fifteen (including no. 30700) made it to 1962 when the class became extinct. Note that the locomotive carries no front numberplate.

5.7.51

Ashford depot had a number of Fairburn 2–6–4Ts working local passenger services during the early fifties. No. 42074 stands ready at Ashford. Note the cleaner in the background polishing the handles on a set of veteran coaches.

1.7.53

Bath depot, shed-code 71G, came within the jurisdiction of the Southern Region, and visitors would usually find at least one or two of the famous Somerset & Dorset Joint Railway 2–8–0s present. All eleven members of the class introduced in 1914 were allocated there. Here no. 53807 stands in the yard with various items on the footplate. The tablet exchange apparatus can be seen on the front of the locomotive tender.

31.8.55

Fresh from works overhaul this is U class 2–6–0 no. 31804 at Exmouth Junction shed. This was one of the engines rebuilt from the SEC K (River) 2–6–4Ts introduced in 1917 following a series of derailments of members of that class. No. 31804 was originally named *River Tamar* and was rebuilt at Brighton Works in 1928.

4.9.56

The W class 2–6–4Ts were a familiar sight at Hither Green depot, where they were used on inter-regional and general freight work. Fifteen members of the class were built and about half were allocated to Hither Green. No. 31912 was to end its days in the scrapyard of Cohens of Kettering, along with two of its classmates.

24.5.56

Another Hither Green W class 2–6–4T no. 31913 stands ready for its next duty alongside King Arthur class no. 30772 *Sir Percivale*.

24.5.56

During the fifties countless photographs must have been taken of the Adams Radial tanks working the Lyme Regis branch. Here no. 30582 is seen leaving Axminster with an afternoon service. All members of the class were built by private companies. No. 30582 was built by R. Stephenson in 1885. It ran over two million miles before being withdrawn in July 1961.

3.9.56

Axminster station with the Lyme Regis bay platform in the foreground. The run-round for the branch engine can be seen together with the water crane and supply tank. The branch service comprised two coaches. On summer Saturdays two engines were required to double-head holiday trains.

3.9.56

Departure time approaches for the afternoon service from Lyme Regis. This picture illustrates the large bunker and sizeable cab fitted to these engines. Note also the gas lamp with its elegant twisted standard. No. 30582, the branch engine at the time of my visit, was sub-shedded at Lyme Regis and changed when it was due for a boiler washout.

3.9.56

The 01 class engines were easily distinguished by their outside-framed tenders. Only a small number remained in service during the early fifties and those that were left were nearing the end of their days and on light duties only. Despite this no. 31064, seen here shunting at Ashford, was in good external condition.

1.7.53

C class no. 31219 awaits its next duty at Ashford. This was one of the first examples of the class to be built at the nearby works. It was completed in December 1900 and remained in service until October 1959. One member was rebuilt in October 1917 as an 0–6–0ST and was used for shunting work at Bricklayers Arms depot in London. It was to become the S class and was withdrawn in September 1951.

1.7.53

In 1953 several of these veteran Wainwright O1 class 0–6–0s with outside-framed tenders were to be found at Ashford. They were rebuilds of a Stirling design introduced in 1876. Among their duties were the Kent & East Sussex services, together with local trains and works shunting. No. 31065 was engaged on this work pushing U1 2–6–0 no. 31899 into position.

1.7.53

Over a hundred of these C class 0–6–0s were taken into British Railways stock in 1948. Introduced by the South Eastern & Chatham Railway in 1900 they were very useful and popular engines and were to be found at numerous sheds in the fifties. Engines of this design were built at Ashford & Longhedge Works and by Neilson, Reid & Sharp Stewart. No. 31711, pictured at Ashford, was one of the class built by Sharp Stewart; completed in 1900 it remained in service until January 1957.

1.7.53

Wainwright C class 0–6–0 no. 31510 was a Gillingham engine. It is seen here at Hither Green shed ready for its return working.

24.5.56

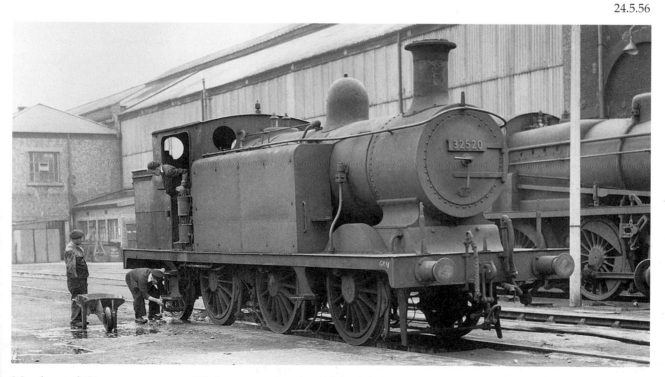

Members of the seventy-strong E4 class were sent to Ashford for overhaul and repairs. The E4s were a London, Brighton & South Coast Railway design, introduced in 1910. Seen here in the yard at Ashford Works no. 32520 appears to have injector trouble.

1.7.53

The repair shop at Bricklayers Arm was usually kept quite busy. Here E3 class no. 32458 awaits attention with the pony truck from a Bulleid Pacific in the foreground. This shed was principally concerned with goods and shunting locomotives working in nearby yards. It closed in June 1962, its remaining engines being transferred to several other sheds.

25.11.54

Shunting work was continually taking place at the busy Ashford shed and this is H class 0–4–4T no. 31523 in action. This engine was fitted for push-pull working. Built in 1909 it had almost completed fifty years' service when it was withdrawn in January 1959.

1.7.53

There was considerable variation within locomotives of the M7 class designed by D. Drummond. No. 30044, seen here at Exmouth Junction, was a typical example. These very useful engines were used on numerous duties in their heyday but in their later years they were a familiar sight working in and out of Waterloo on empty stock.

4.9.56

The 02 class was first introduced by W. Adams in 1889 for light suburban services. All were built at Nine Elms Works. No. 30179 is seen here awaiting attention at Eastleigh. It remained in traffic until December 1959. Twenty-three members of this class were used for many years on the Isle of Wight, where they all carried local names.

8.11.55

The E4 class 0–6–2Ts were powerful engines and were to be found at numerous depots in the Southern Region. The London Brighton & South Coast Railway first introduced them in 1910 to the design of R.J. Billinton. Seventy were in service in the early fifties, plus four more classified E4X which had been rebuilt with larger boilers. No. 32491 was photographed at its home shed, Eastleigh.

8.11.55

The two diminutive C14 class 0–4–0Ts allocated to Eastleigh depot were used at Southampton Town Quay for shunting work. No. 30589 was the spare engine when this picture was taken. These engines were rebuilds by Urie of Drummond 2–2–0Ts built for rail-motor use. A third locomotive, no. 77S, was used at Redbridge sleeper depot.

8.11.55

Several of the R1 class 0–6–0Ts were fitted with cut down boiler mountings for working the Whitstable branch. Here no. 31010, with the round-type Stirling cab, is engaged on shunting work at Ashford. The R1s, as a class, will be best remembered in the post-war period for working boat-trains on the Folkestone Harbour branch.

1.7.53

During 1927/8 the ten locomotives that comprised the E1/R class were rebuilds by R.E.L. Maunsell of Stroudley E1 0–6–0Ts introduced in 1874 principally for working passenger services in the West Country. No. 32697 was employed on routine shed pilot duties at Exmouth Junction depot when this picture was taken.

4.9.56

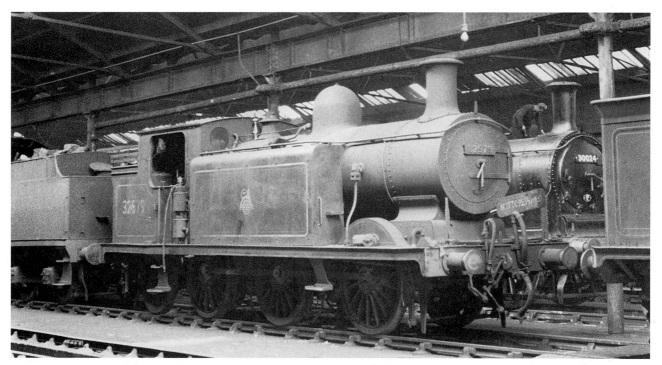

E4 class no. 32579 under repair in Eastleigh shed. The frequently seen 'not to be moved' plate on the buffer beam can be clearly seen. In the background M7 no. 30024, fresh from works overhaul, is receiving attention from one of the depot's fitters.

8.11.55

This lightweight 2MT 2–6–2T design was introduced by Ivatt for the LMS in 1946, along with his 2–6–0 design. Both were very successful with construction continuing into British Railways days. In due course examples were to be found in several regions. No. 41300, completed in 1952, was one of four allocated to Bricklayers Arms depot. It managed just twelve years' service.

24.11.54

Busy times at Ryde Pier head as 02 class 0–4–4T no. 21 *Sandown* gets ready to leave. Another of its classmates would follow shortly afterwards. Twenty-five members of the 02 class were on the Isle of Wight together with four E1 class 0–6–0Ts. One example, no. 24 *Calbourne*, is in preservation on the island.

11.9.59

In 1929 the first of the eight Z class 0–8–0Ts came into service. These were designed to work in the principal goods yards. They were sturdy and powerful locomotives and were well liked by enginemen. Several were to be found at Exmouth Junction, including no. 30950. In the fifties it was employed on banking trains and shunting duties.

4.9.56

Stratford depot J19 no. 64665 had worked through to the Southern Region with a freight train and is pictured here standing at Hither Green shed ready for its return working. The J19s were introduced in 1912 and later rebuilt with round-topped boilers which gave them a much more modern appearance.

24.5.56

Heavy rain and wind greeted me when I arrived at Wadebridge shed but it did not stop me photographing the famous Beattie 2–4–0WTs, two of which were working that day. No. 30586 was on shunting work, while the third was spare and in the shed. In the background is a tender from a T9 class 4–4–0; these engines worked many local services including the Padstow branch.

5.9.56

During the fifties both the Western and Southern Regions had locomotive depots in Plymouth. The Southern Region shed 72D was known as Plymouth Friary. Among its allocation were a number of B4 class 0–4–0Ts used for dock shunting. No. 30094, seen here not long after a general overhaul, was among them. Note the rather tatty spark arrester. Four West Country class Pacifics were also to be found at the depot.

5.9.56

The London Midland Region

Within the huge area covered by this region were several cities and many large towns, including the industrial areas of the north. The principal passenger locomotives were the Princess Coronation class. These Pacifics were rated 8P, and most were based at LMR depots with a handful north of the border. In addition there were thirteen examples of the Princess Royal class that Stanier introduced in 1933, five years before his very successful Princess Coronations (widely referred to as 'Duchesses'). One of the Princess Royals, built in 1935, was an experimental turbine-driven engine. Unlike all the others it remained un-named. In 1952 it was rebuilt as a conventional locomotive, but was short-lived in this form as it was damaged beyond repair in the Harrow crash in the following October. Other passenger engines in the region were the Royal Scot and Jubilee classes, both of 4–6–0 wheel arrangement.

Every region had a mixed traffic design that was used on all work. In the case of the London Midland Region it was Stanier's class 5 4–6–0, commonly known as 'Black Fives'. For heavy freight the famous 8F 2–8–0s were the principal goods locomotives. A considerable number of London & North Western 0–8–0s were still active, some lasting into the sixties. While they did not have a particularly sheltered cab for the enginemen they were powerful engines, albeit at times emitting rather peculiar almost asthmatic sounds as they got to grips with their trains.

The former Midland Railway was well represented, its 0–6–0T shunting tank being continued as a post-Grouping development. It became the standard LMS shunting design. There were 417 in service at this time. The Compounds and 2P 4–4–0s were still frequently seen in the early years of the decade, but from the mid-fifties their duties were taken over by more modern engines and diesel power.

If there is one locomotive that will remain forever in my memory it is the famous 'Lickey Banker'. This massive 0–10–0 engine spent its working life pounding up the famous incline. I was fortunate to see, and photograph, this unique engine at work.

Jubilee no. 45576 *Bombay* heads through Bletchley carrying reporting number W566. The rolling stock of this parcel train was quite a mixture. The second vehicle, a full brake, was of straight-sided type. Bletchley locomotive depot was on the left of the picture, behind the parcels van.

21.8.54

Running on clear signals Class 5 no. 45326, a Carnforth engine, is about to pass through Bletchley with an express. On the right can be seen the Bedford line. Note also the tall signal posts on both Up and Down lines.

21.8.54

Crab no. 42730, pictured at a rather wet Bury shed, had recently worked a special (or was about to do so). These engines were instantly recognisable by their raised running plate, inclined cylinders and rather distinctive chimney. No. 42730 managed just over thirty years' service. Completed in May 1931, it was withdrawn in July 1961.

22.9.57

Unfortunately I only had one opportunity to photograph the famous Lickey Banker, no. 58100, at work. This was on a Sunday morning as it banked a heavy express from Bristol headed by a Class 5. This massive 0–10–0 was built in 1919 and spent its entire working life blasting up the incline.

17.5.55

As at many London Midland Region depots, Class 5s were well to the fore at Northampton, although no. 45252 was a visitor from Warrington. Northampton was an average size depot with over thirty engines. It closed in 1965.

5.9.54

The small sub-shed at Lincoln St Marks came under the jurisdiction of the Eastern Region depot 40A Lincoln. Here 2P no. 40552 is moving forwards to take water. This engine was allocated to Nottingham at this time.

26.8.51

Several Compounds were allocated to Trafford Park depot but by 1957 work for them had become very scarce and a number were standing in various parts of the shed yard. No. 41170 looks ready for action, coaled and watered, but it had in fact already been withdrawn.
22.9.57

Once a proud express, locomotive D11 no. 62661 *Gerard Powys Dewhurst* presented a sad sight at Trafford Park. The chimney had been sheeted down, a common practice at the time. Despite this the engine was returned to traffic and finally withdrawn in November 1960.
22.9.57

Another Compound standing idle at Trafford Park was no. 41116, which was in poor external condition. It seems unlikely that it ever worked again, as it was withdrawn three months after this picture was taken. No. 41116 was one of the post-Grouping locomotives completed in July 1925.
22.9.57

Standing at Bournville depot between two massive coal dumps are Compound no. 41180, a Fowler 2–6–4T and a 3F 0–6–0. The Compound was one of the post-Grouping engines and was completed in December 1925. When this picture was taken work was already becoming scarce for these engines. No. 41180 was withdrawn from service in March 1957.

17.5.55

Six 3-cylinder Compounds were still allocated to Bedford in the early fifties and were used principally on St Pancras services. By 1954 time was running out as their duties were being taken over by the Standard designs. No. 41049 was photographed arriving back at its home depot having recently worked back from London.

11.9.54

The massive 2–6–6–2T Beyer Garratt locomotives were a familiar sight on the Midland main line, hauling heavy mineral trains. In all thirty-three were in service, and all except two had revolving coal bunkers, as seen here. Introduced in 1927 these engines were a Fowler & Beyer Peacock design for the LMS. No. 47968 had run into trouble at Wellingborough.

27.3.55

Kettering depot was adjacent to the Up slow station platform so it was quite easy to see most of what was on shed. These 8Fs, nos 48356 and 48360, were principally employed on working iron ore traffic from the Northamptonshire quarries that were still active in the early fifties.

31.5.52

Oxford was one of those places where you could see locomotives from four regions, especially in the summer months. This 8F 2–8–0 no. 48754 had not travelled far though, as it was a Bletchley engine. It was photographed moving on shed to take coal and water ready to work a goods train back. The passenger services between Oxford and Bletchley were mostly in the hands of Class 5 4–6–0s.

31.10.54

The LMS 7F 0–8–0s were a development of the well-known LNWR heavy goods engines. They were never very popular and by the fifties the remaining engines were all to be found at northern sheds. No. 49560 was photographed at Bolton when it had only three months left in service.

22.9.57

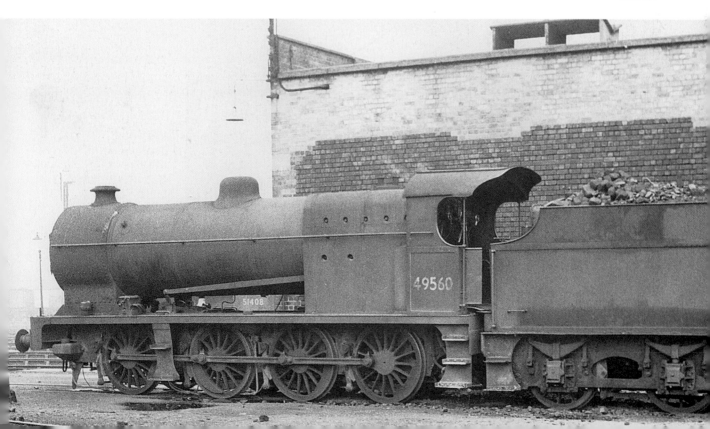

The twelve LNWR 0–8–0s allocated to Bletchley were used on local goods trains on the main line, on sand trains from Leighton Buzzard and occasionally on workings to Cambridge via Sandy. No. 49330, pictured here at Bletchley, was a visitor from Nuneaton. This was a sizeable shed, having eighteen of these locomotives in the mid-fifties.

21.8.54

The chimney of LNWR 0–8–0 no. 49105, pictured at Northampton, had seen better days. This engine was built at Crewe Works and was completed in May 1910 as a G class 2-cylinder 0–8–0. In October 1936 it was converted to a G1 and in 1939 to a 62A. These engines were well liked and powerful but had rather spartan cab conditions.

5.9.54

Class 4F no. 44133 of Toton shed ambles along the main line at Bedford with a lightweight goods. The engine was still fitted with one of the distinctive Midland-type chimneys. It was one of the large batch completed in 1927 and was withdrawn in March 1963.

21.8.54

The 4F 0–6–0 design was first introduced by Fowler for the Midland Railway in 1911, and a post-Grouping development followed in 1924. In the early fifties the class consisted of 762 locomotives allocated to various depots in the London Midland and Scottish Regions. No. 43876, seen here at Bedford, is a typical example of the Midland design. In the background is one of the more numerous post-Grouping engines.

11.9.54

Class 4F no. 44297 of Cricklewood depot takes water at Bedford. This locomotive was completed in February 1927 and remained in service until August 1963. It was fitted with automatic train control for working over LTS lines. Part of this equipment can be seen mounted in front of the cab.

11.9.54

The fireman of 3F no. 43313 operates the points as the engine moves on shed. The weekends were a good time to catch the locomotives used for brickworks, shunting and trip work as they were usually on shed. It was very different during the week as only those stopped for repairs or maintenance were present.

21.8.54

The 3F 0–6–0s allocated to Bedford were mostly used for shunting work at the surrounding brickworks. No. 43785 is an example of the Deeley Midland Railway design introduced in 1906 and later rebuilt by Fowler with a Belpaire boiler. This engine, which was at Bedford for many years, is seen here heading for the water crane.

21.8.54

Another visitor to Northampton was 3F 0–6–0 no. 43399 from Nottingham. It is seen here between two of the depots LNWR 0–8–0s. Five members of this class were allocated to the shed with several others based nearby, including at Bletchley and Rugby.

5.9.54

From 1911 onwards several members of the Lancashire & Yorkshire Railway 0–6–0s were rebuilt with Belpaire boilers and extended smokeboxes. No. 52431 of Bolton shed was one of these rebuilt engines; behind it is one of the conventional members of the class that was introduced in 1889.

16.10.55

The section of the line between Huntingdon East and St Ives was single track, the only passing-place being at Godmanchester station. Here 2MT no. 46444 has just arrived with the afternoon Kettering–Cambridge service and already has the token. The goods train in the background will now get the right away.

7.6.52

The J10 class 0–6–0s were to be found at many northern depots. No. 65153, pictured here at Trafford Park, was officially classified J10/4. These were a development of the earlier J10/2 engines introduced by Pollitt in 1896, the most obvious change being the larger tenders. No. 65153 was built by Beyer Peacock & Company in 1896 and remained in service until December 1956.

22.9.57

In 1901 Robinson introduced a further batch of these useful engines that were classified J10/6. These had larger bearings and smaller tenders. No. 65181, seen here at Trafford Park, was an example. It was completed in July 1901 at Gorton Works and ended its service in November 1956. Note the tender spectacle plate.

22.9.57

Bedford depot had just one example of the well-known 2F 0–6–0 design, no. 58305. The engine still retained the old-type cab but had been rebuilt with a Belpaire boiler. Judging from its appearance it had recently received a works overhaul, as the chimney and smokebox have been repainted.

11.9.54

Jinty 3F 0–6–0s were widespread throughout the London Midland Region as they were the standard LMS shunting locomotive. No. 47521, seen here at Bletchley, was unusual in that it was not carrying a front numberplate. In the early fifties 427 examples of this class were at work. Introduced in 1924, they were a post-Grouping development of a much earlier Midland design.

5.9.54

Only one example of the Stanier 3MT 2–6–2T design, no. 40165, was allocated to Bedford. At weekends it was usually present in the sidings outside the depot. This engine was completed in November 1937 and remained in service until October 1961. Other locomotives in this picture are a 2F 0–6–0, a 4F 0–6–0 and a Standard 4MT 2–6–4T.

11.9.54

There was considerable variation to be found among the ex-Lancashire & Yorkshire Railway 2–4–2Ts remaining in the fifties. No. 50850, photographed at Bolton, had longer tanks and increased coal capacity, a Belpaire boiler and an extended smokebox. Many of the duties once worked by these engines had already been taken over by more modern locomotives.

22.9.57

You wouldn't expect to find ex-Lancashire & Yorkshire Railway 2–4–2Ts a long way from their home territory. No. 50650 was one of those allocated to Wellingborough during the mid-fifties. This shed was not very good for photography as most engines were to be found in the gloomy confines of the roundhouse, but in spite of this I did manage to get this shot of the engine.

22.7.56

The ex-Lancashire & Yorkshire Railway 0–6–0STs started life as Class 23 0–6–0 tender engines first introduced in 1876. Rebuilding to saddle tanks commenced in 1891 under the direction of J. Aspinall and well over seventy were in service in the early fifties, all based at northern sheds. No. 51486 is pictured here at a gloomy Bolton depot accompanied by Compound no. 40937.

22.9.57

Trafford Park depot was home to a mixture of locomotives of LMS and LNER classification. This engine, 2–6–4T no. 42469, was a typical example of the Stanier taper-boiler 2-cylinder design introduced in 1935. It was photographed on the shed road coupled to wagons used to transport ash. Two locomotives of the type were allocated here in the early fifties together with others introduced by Fairburn.

22.9.57

The Eastern Region

I lived for many years near the East Coast main line and my most outstanding memory is, without question, of the famous Gresley Pacifics, not just the top-link A4s heading the principal expresses but also the A3s. Great excitement was always aroused among local enthusiasts when one from a depot north of the border or from Carlisle worked through – a rare event. The only chance of this happening was when they were running-in fresh from Doncaster Works, and they came south of Peterborough only on very odd occasions. One train that was often worked by a running-in turn was a parcels which arrived in London in the very early hours of the morning. Another engine with which I became very familiar was the unique streamlined W1 4–6–4 that made almost daily appearances during the fifties.

Apart from the 9F 2–10–0s, Standard designs were rare on the main line south of Peterborough until Britannias displaced from duties in East Anglia took over the Kings Cross–Cleethorpes service, replacing the immaculate Immingham depot B1s on this train. Countless enthusiasts were drawn to Cambridge by the E4 2–4–0s, as most of the survivors were allocated there. Their work included the Colne Valley services and carriage pilot duties, and during the early fifties it was quite usual to see two or more at work. These were the last 2–4–0 tender engines in service on British Railways. There were a considerable number of ex-Great Eastern 0–6–0Ts still active well into the fifties, as well as 2–4–2Ts of classes F4, F5 and F6. As the fifties progressed many of these were to make their last journey to Stratford Works, with some of the survivors spending a considerable time in store.

The Great Central Railway was mainly represented by three classes, the sturdy reliable 2–8–0s classified O4, the very useful J11 class 0–6–0s, widely known as 'Pom Poms', and the N5 class 0–6–2Ts which were well distributed especially at depots that were at one time part of the Great Central.

Anyone who was familiar with Kings Cross in the early and mid-fifties will doubtless remember the sturdy N2 class 0–6–2Ts that worked suburban services and also acted as station pilots. The earlier N1 0–6–2Ts were still to be found in the London area together with J52 0–6–0STs and J50 0–6–0Ts. On a journey in and out of Kings Cross you would invariably see a considerable number quietly going about their duties.

The locomotives mentioned are only a small selection of what was around. The Eastern also had its one-offs, such as the W1 already mentioned. The massive 2–8–8–2T banker no. 69999 classified U1, like its counterpart on the London Midland, the 'Lickey Banker' no. 58100 'Big Bertha', spent its working life on banking duties.

The 'Plant Centenarian' heads south near Huntingdon with two veteran Atlantics in full cry. Two specials using these engines were run to commemorate Doncaster Works. Leading is no. 990 *Henry Oakley*, built in 1898, the first of a class of twenty-two. It was withdrawn in 1937, restored and sent to York Railway Museum. No. 251, the first large Atlantic, was built in 1902 and withdrawn in 1947, receiving the same treatment. On this day the locomotives were in the very capable hands of two Kings Cross top-link drivers. No. 990 was doing most of the work as the superheater had been removed from no. 251, resulting in impaired steam ability.

26.9.53

The legendary 'Flying Scotsman' is seen here going in fine style on an enthusiasts' special near Huntingdon. The train is the Westminster Bank Railway Society Special to York, composed of Gresley stock. No. 60103 was a Grantham engine which had returned to the East Coast main line after a spell on the Great Central, allocated to Leicester GC depot.

3.4.55

A3 no. 60067 *Ladas* heads a Kings Cross to Peterborough train at Huntingdon. The usual motive power at this time would have been a B1 4–6–0 or an L1 2–6–4T from Hitchin depot.

6.7.52

In the early fifties the W1 no. 60700 was a Kings Cross engine. It is seen here leaving Huntingdon with the Sunday Kings Cross–Peterborough semi-fast. The engine was later transferred to Doncaster but was still a familiar sight each day at Kings Cross.

14.8.52

In 1945 Edward Thompson rebuilt Gresley A1 no. 4470 *Great Northern* to A1/1. Very little of the original engine was retained, and even the frames were completely new. When *Great Northern* emerged from Doncaster Works it was sent to Kings Cross. By the time this picture was taken at Doncaster it was a Grantham engine. Most of the locomotive's later life was spent on semi-fasts. Withdrawal took place in November 1962.

25.8.57

During the fifties several locomotive types worked the afternoon service from Kings Cross. Here A2/3 no. 60500 *Edward Thompson* of New England depot is in charge, still at this time with a plain chimney. Later L1 and B1 locomotives became the normal motive power for this service.

29.7.52

A4 no. 60025 *Falcon* in immaculate condition heads north from Huntingdon with the Sunday morning three-coach semi-fast from Kings Cross, before returning to London on an express. This service was worked by A1s, A2s, A3s and A4s and sometimes by a V2 2–6–2.

3.8.52

V2 class no. 60867 of Doncaster shed working hard with a mixed train of empty passenger stock near Abbots Ripton. The third coach appears to be a very interesting example, being of lower height than the others.

3.10.53

Cambridge depot had a stud of B1 4–6–0s that worked services to Liverpool Street and Kings Cross among their other duties. The B1s were well maintained and popular with enginemen. No. 61333 was one of those built by the North British Locomotive Company. Completed after nationalisation in July 1948, it was withdrawn in December 1962.

17.5.52

B1 class locomotives were built at British Railways' Darlington and Gorton Works, as well as by the North British Locomotive Company and Vulcan Foundry. No. 61097, seen here at Cambridge, was completed by the North British Locomotive Company in November 1946 and remained in service until January 1965. In all 410 B1s were built.

17.5.52

The afternoon parcels at St Ives headed by Sandringham B17 class no. 61619 *Welbeck Abbey* of March depot. This duty was normally worked by a Claud, and only occasionally by a Sandringham. The rather faded station noticeboard reads 'St Ives change for Godmanchester and Huntingdon'. All traces of this station and line have long since gone.

8.9.54

K3 class no. 61804 of New England shed heads down the 1-in-200 incline from Abbots Ripton with a fast goods bound for London. K3s were common on the main line during the early fifties, and included locomotives from Immingham depot working fish trains. In due course most of these duties were taken over by B1 class 4–6–0s.

20.7.52

Passenger services on the St Ives loop were sparse, as the line was principally used for goods trains avoiding the line from March to Cambridge. The afternoon service usually stood in the station for several minutes before heading off to Cambridge. D16/3 no. 62551 sports a typical headcode disc.

7.6.52

For most of the fifties the Claud Hamilton D16 class 4–4–0s handled local traffic in East Anglia although they also worked into London Midland territory. Until the mid-fifties no. 62585 of Cambridge was a regular engine on the Bletchley service. No. 62574, pictured at St Ives, was heading the afternoon Kings Lynn–Cambridge service.

8.9.54

The Robinson Great Central 04 class introduced in 1911 is unquestionably among the classic locomotive designs. In addition to being built for the Great Central they were also produced in large numbers for the government during the First World War. They were constructed by four separate private companies, with the North British Locomotive Company building the highest numbers. In due course examples were to find their way to many far distant countries, and a few saw wartime service in the Middle East. After the war the LNER took 273 of these engines into stock, including N4 no. 63823, pictured here at Ardsley. Built by the North British Locomotive Company in October 1918, it was rebuilt as an 04/8 in October 1957 and withdrawn in August 1962.

13.5.56

J39 class no. 64911 in charge of a works train at Ardsley while engineering work was in progress. The J39s, introduced by Gresley in 1926, were a class that quietly went about their duties attracting little attention. There were 289 members of the class, the only variation being in the type of tender fitted. No. 64911 had one of the LNER standard type.

13.5.56

Two views of 04/3 no. 63864 at Ardsley in September 1957. This 04 was among the ex-government locomotives purchased by the LNER, and it entered traffic in August 1925. No. 63864 was one of the large number constructed by the North British Locomotive Company. It was completed in August 1919, several months after the war had ended. Later converted to an 04/8, it was withdrawn from service in August 1962.

13.5.56

There was a steady stream of goods trains in both directions at St Ives. Here J19 no. 64661 heads for its home depot, March. The J19s were originally introduced to the design of S. Holden for the Great Eastern Railway. From 1934 onwards they were rebuilt with round-topped boilers.

7.6.52

It wasn't often that the opportunity arose to photograph the Huntingdon East pilot broadside as it was normally alongside the small coal stage. No. 65461 was a Cambridge engine, and it worked the ten-day roster as pilot at Huntingdon. Two sets of enginemen worked from the small sub-shed.

1.6.52

The last member of the fifteen-strong J1 class, no. 65013 was allocated to Hitchin depot. Built in 1908 for the Great Northern Railway to the design of H.A. Ivatt, these engines were used on mixed traffic duties, their 5ft 8in driving wheels giving them a fair turn of speed. No. 65013 is seen here at Huntingdon on ballast train duties. It spent most of its last months in service on this duty. On several occasions the gallant little locomotive was used on local trains from Hitchin to Kings Cross. It was withdrawn in November 1954.

9.9.54

Stratford L1 no. 67729 stands at the head of a train of close-coupled suburban stock at Cambridge. E. Thompson introduced the L1s in 1945, and in all a hundred examples were built.

17.5.52

For a while L1 class tank locomotives from Hitchin depot were used on Kings Cross to Peterborough local services before handing over to B1 4–6–0s from the same shed. Here no. 67734 starts away from Huntingdon with an afternoon service to Peterborough.

17.6.52

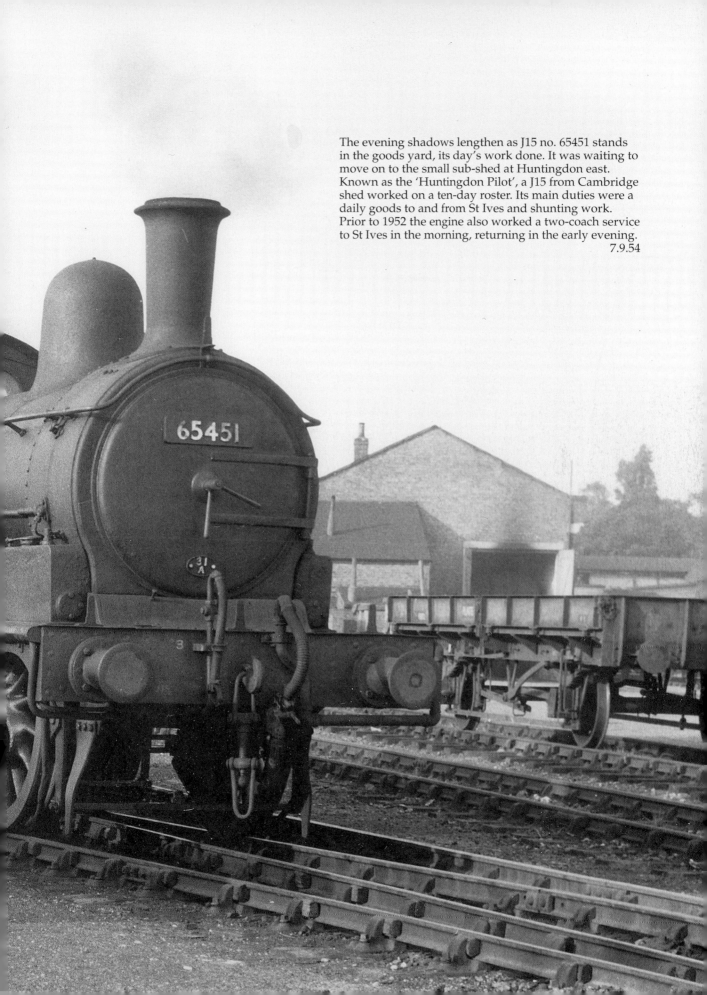

The evening shadows lengthen as J15 no. 65451 stands in the goods yard, its day's work done. It was waiting to move on to the small sub-shed at Huntingdon east. Known as the 'Huntingdon Pilot', a J15 from Cambridge shed worked on a ten-day roster. Its main duties were a daily goods to and from St Ives and shunting work. Prior to 1952 the engine also worked a two-coach service to St Ives in the morning, returning in the early evening.

7.9.54

Hitchin depot provided motive power for a pick-up goods that ran to and from Huntingdon. Here L1 class 2–6–4T no. 67799 waits to cross over the Up slow to commence its return journey. Other classes that worked this train were J6 0–6–0s and for a short time Fowler 2–6–4Ts on loan from the London Midland Region.

7.9.54

Travelling on the East Coast main line in the early fifties you would have seen J52s busy in most of the marshalling yards. A large number were based in the London area. No. 68885 was a Doncaster engine, pictured here at its home shed. Note the poor external condition – its locomotive number can barely be seen through the dirt and grime.

25.8.57

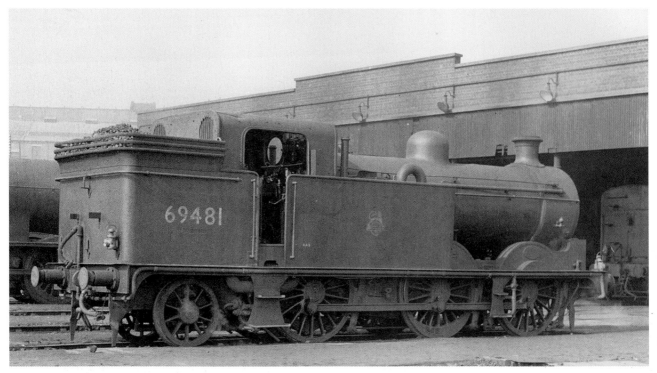

Examples of the ex-Great Northern N1 class were still to be found in the London area during the early fifties. Others were allocated to depots in the West Riding of Yorkshire. No. 69481 was one of these, pictured here at Copley Hill shed.

13.5.56

The North Eastern Region

The locomotives from this region that travelled most widely in steam days were the B16 class 4–6–0s, along with the Pacifics and V2s. Occasionally working through to London, the B16s were also familiar on the former Great Central territory. They were mostly from York shed, which had a considerable number in its allocation. The region also had a large number of 0–8–0s for handling the heavy mineral traffic. The most numerous were the very reliable Q6 0–8–0s, a design introduced by Raven in 1913. In all the class numbered 120. In 1919 Raven introduced his much more powerful Q7 class. Only fifteen of these were built, and by 1954 all were allocated to Tyne Dock shed where their duties included the Tyne Dock to Consett iron ore trains.

By the mid-fifties work was not as plentiful for the large T1 class 4–8–0Ts; although those at York were normally to be seen in steam, some of the Newport allocation were already in store. Examples of the large A8 4–6–2Ts were to be found at a number of North Eastern depots, where they were mainly used on local passenger work. These engines started life as 4–4–4Ts, being rebuilt by Gresley from 1931 onwards.

Although the North East Region did not have one of the largest steam allocations, it still had plenty of interest to offer the enthusiast.

The well-proportioned lines of A3 no. 60046 *Diamond Jubilee* can be clearly seen in this picture of the locomotive taken at Copley Hill shed, Leeds. This engine ended its working life at Grantham shed in company with several of its classmates. It was withdrawn in July 1963 and cut up at Doncaster.

3.5.56

Only a comparatively small number of the 410-strong B1 class were named, forty of them after species of antelope. One such was no. 61019 *Nilghai*, photographed here at Stockton. This was a Darlington-built engine. Completed in February 1947, it remained in service until March 1967.

8.7.56

Darlington Works was responsible for overhauling the entire D49 class in British Railways days. Examples were to be found in both the North Eastern and Scottish Regions. No. 62716 *Kincardineshire* had arrived for maintenance and was on Darlington shed when photographed.

8.7.56

By the mid-fifties there was little general work for the few remaining North Eastern Railway D20 class engines, although summer excursions and specials were to see most of them back in action. Worsdell introduced the D20 class in 1899, and they were superheated during their long service. Here no. 62386 stands at Selby depot.

23.9.56

Someone had just cleaned part of the front numberplate of A8 4–6–2 no. 69862. These massive tank locomotives were rebuilds of V. Raven 4–4–4Ts, first introduced in 1913 but not suited to the steeply graded lines of the north-east. Rebuilding to the highly successful six-coupled design commenced in 1931 to the design of Nigel Gresley. No. 69862 was an early withdrawal, going in July 1958.

8.7.56

Two of the massive T1 class 4–8–0Ts stand ready for duty inside the smoky confines of York depot. Work was already becoming scarce for these engines, with several examples in store at other sheds. The T1 class consisted of thirteen engines, introduced in 1909 by W. Worsdell for the North Eastern Railway.

13.5.56

Fresh from general overhaul and resplendent in lined-out livery V1, no. 67618 stands ready to return to its home depot north of the border at Polmadie. Many of the V1 class had already been rebuilt to V3, but this did not happen to no. 67618 until September 1958. It had four more years in service.

8.7.56.

This view of 01 no. 63856 on the Tyne Dock–Consett iron ore train shows one of the 56-ton bogie wagons in more detail. The two Westinghouse pumps on the locomotive can be clearly seen.

7.7.56

In the mid-fifties Middlesbrough depot had an allocation of just over sixty locomotives, including nineteen Q6 class 0–8–0s. here no. 63368 is seen in company with Ivatt 2–6–0 no. 43073 in the open roundhouse with the docks behind. When the depot closed in June 1958 all its locomotives were transferred to the new depot at Thornaby.

8.7.56

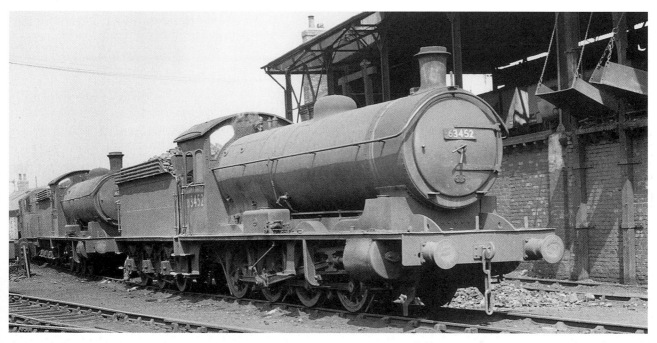

Two of Middlesbrough depot's stud of Q6 0–8–0s standing near the massive coaling plant. This class was widely used in the area working to and from the collieries. All 120 members of this powerful class were fitted with steam brake only. No. 63452, seen here, was built by Armstrong Whitworth in 1920 and withdrawn in April 1963.

8.7.56

In 1952 five 01 class 2–8–0s were fitted with Westinghouse pumps and vacuum ejectors for working the Tyne Dock–Consett iron ore block-trains. The pumps were necessary to operate the 56-ton bogie wagon doors. No. 63856 is seen here at Tyne Docks. This engine remained in service until November 1962.

7.7.56

No. 65754, pictured at Newport, was one of the Q6 class built at the North Eastern Railway's Darlington Works in 1905. Work had evidently been taking place in the depot yard at Newport, as wheelbarrows, sleepers and tools are lying around. This engine was among the first of the class to be withdrawn, being condemned in June 1958.

8.7.56

The J27 class was first introduced by the North Eastern Railway in 1904 to the design of W. Worsdell. Initially construction took place at Darlington, moving on to Gateshead Works in 1905. No. 65740 was completed at Darlington in 1904. Note the three coal rails on the tender; others had two or four. No. 65740 was withdrawn in January 1959.

8.7.56

Every British Railways region relied heavily on examples of 0–6–0 designs. Most handled goods workings but in some cases they were also commonplace on passenger duties. In their early days the J26 class engines were principally employed over long distances on heavy mineral and freight workings. By the fifties many of their duties were trip workings to and from collieries. The largest concentration of the fifty-strong class was at Newport where this picture of no. 65740 was taken.

8.7.56

Some of the numerous lines near Neville Hill shed can be seen in this picture of J27 no. 65793. Work appears to be in progress on the track as no ballast can be seen between the sleepers. The J27 was the last of several North Eastern 0–6–0 classes to be introduced.

13.5.56

During the fifties many enthusiasts were principally concerned with locomotive numbers. In this picture taken at Neville Hill shed a small group can be seen standing in front of J25 no. 65654. On the right of the picture a locomotive has been connected to the turntable equipment prior to moving off shed.

13.5.56

The twenty-strong class of N10 0–6–2Ts were built at Darlington Works in 1902/3. They were long lived, the last remaining in service until 1962. No. 69106 is seen here in Tyne Dock in company with J72.

7.7.56

N10 class no. 69104 stands at Hull Dairycoates depot with steam leaking from several places. This engine was built at the North Eastern Railway's Darlington Works in 1902 to the design of W. Worsdell. The N10s were powerful goods tank locomotives. This example remained in service until March 1958.

22.5.55

Locomotives awaiting works were usually to be seen in the yards at Darlington shed. J71 no. 68296, built in 1892, was also fitted with dumb buffers for moving chaldron wagons; these can be clearly seen inside those of standard pattern. Behind the J71 is a very work-stained class A8 4–6–2T also awaiting entry into the works.

8.7.56

During the 1950s the York station pilots and shunting locomotives used York South depot, where J71 class no. 68280 awaits its next duty. This locomotive was one of the few members of the class equipped to work passenger stock. Built at Darlington in 1892, it completed sixty-five years in service.

8.7.56

J77 class locomotives were built at Darlington, Gateshead and York, as well as by Neilson & Co. and Hawthorn & Co. Withdrawals started in 1933, with only forty-six of the once sixty-strong class being taken over by British Railways in 1948. The J77s started life in 1874 as 0–4–4Ts. No. 68423, seen here at Darlington, was built at Gateshead in 1878. Rebuilt at York in 1902, it remained in service until November 1957.

8.7.56

A rare opportunity in splendid light conditions to photograph J72 no. 69001 arriving at Hull Dairycoates, fresh from works. Note in particular the spotless wheels, with no trace of oil and grime. How long would they have remained in this condition? This was one of the engines sub-shedded at Alexandra Dock.

22.5.55

During the fifties members of the J94 class were to be found at several North Eastern Region depots. Newport, where this picture of no. 68011 was taken, had seven. This engine was one of the batch built by the Hunslet Engine Company in 1944. Withdrawals started in 1960, with no. 68011 soldiering on until May 1965.

8.7.56

The J94 engines were designed by Riddles for the War Department, the first being completed in 1943. During 1946/7 the LNER purchased seventy-five, which had been built by six different companies. Modifications included an additional footstep midway along the running plate, together with additional handrails. The majority were also fitted with extended bunkers. J94 class no. 68060, pictured here at Newport, was built by Hudswell Clark & Company in 1945, and remained in service until May 1965.

8.7.56

The Scottish Region

I well remember my first visit to Scotland and seeing many unfamiliar classes for the first time, to say nothing of the strange but intriguing names carried by some of the passenger locomotives! There were also of course numerous designs with which I was very familiar.

Edinburgh, with its nearby docks, was a 'must' to visit. Among the locomotives used for shunting here were a number of Y9 class 0–4–0STs with permanently attached ancient-looking wooden tenders. These engines were first introduced in 1882 by the North British Railway, and were ideal for work on lines with tight curves.

During the fifties tender locomotives of the 4–4–0 wheel arrangement were still a very familiar sight on all regions except the Western Region which had only a small number. In all the others 4–4–0s were widely used on semi-fast, secondary, cross-country and local passenger workings. The Scottish Region was certainly no exception. Those which were at one time in LNER ownership mostly carried names. The D11/2s known as 'Scottish Directors' were a post-Grouping development built to the Scottish loading gauge. These all carried names that were very strange-sounding to enthusiasts from south of the border, such as *Luckie*, *Mucklebackit*, *Bailie MacWheeble* and *Edie Ochiltree*. Many of the D30s were also named after individuals, while the D34s carried names of Scottish glens. In the north the former Great North of Scotland Railway D40s were the last survivors of several designs built for this company, a handful of which carried names. There were also a sizeable number of Gresley D49s working in Scotland.

In addition a considerable number of 4–4–0s, once part of the LMS, were to be seen in the region, including those of Caledonian Railway origin having the power classification 3P. None was named. The last of the Highland Railway 'Bens' was at one time considered for preservation but sadly it was eventually cut up after a long period in storage. Also to be found at Scottish sheds were Compounds and 2P 4–4–0s, both designs originating from the Midland Railway with construction of post-Grouping developments going on into LMS days.

A great many other Scottish engines were not found south of the border. These ranged from Gresley K4 2–6–0s built for the West Highland line to the two V4 class 2–6–2s, one of which was named *Bantam Cock* while the other, no. 61701, was un-named. At Aberdeen docks four small 0–4–2Ts of classes Z4 and Z5, built for the Great North of Scotland Railway in 1915, were still working. There were many other equally interesting classes to be seen in the region, many of which appear in the following selection of photographs.

Two of Haymarket's stud of A4 Pacifics: nearest the camera is no. 60009 *Union of South Africa* with no. 60004 *William Whitelaw* alongside. Note the burnished buffers and cylinder ends. One buffer on no. 60009 had been removed for attention. Fortunately *Union of South Africa* has survived into preservation.

22.8.55

For many years the four A3s allocated to Carlisle Canal depot remained unchanged. These locomotives were mostly confined to the Waverley route, and were only seen at Doncaster when they were due for works overhaul. This was frustrating for enthusiasts further south, whose only chance of seeing them was on Doncaster running-in turns. No. 60079 *Bayardo* was photographed at Haymarket shed.

22.8.55

The ash-pits at Aberdeen Ferryhill depot on a grey foggy morning with A2 class no. 60525 *A.H. Peppercorn* receiving attention. Note the number of tools lying around. Three A2 Pacifics were allocated to the shed in the mid-fifties.

24.8.55

St Margaret's was the largest Scottish depot with over 220 locomotives on its books in the mid-fifties. It occupied a large area on both sides of the running lines. Here a row of V2s await their next duty with no. 60886 from Gateshead shed nearest the camera.

21.8.55

In the mid-fifties D30/2 class no. 62420 *Dominie Sampson* was one of the eight members of the class allocated to the depot. It is seen here at St Margaret's depot awaiting attention before it could work back to its home depot. The D30s had long been familiar in the Edinburgh area and elsewhere in Scotland.

21.8.55

The cripple siding at Haymarket with D30 class no. 62436 *Lord Glenvarloch* minus its front set of driving wheels. Behind is A3 no. 60090 *Grand Parade* also undergoing repairs. The D30 was a Dunfermline engine. Note the smokebox door with its signs of hard work.

22.8.55

One of the fitters at Thornton Junction depot takes a close look at D30 class no. 62429 *The Abbot*. In the background is the massive coaling plant that was in frequent use at this busy depot. Thornton had a sizeable allocation of ex-North British 4–4–0s of classes D30 and D34.

23.8.55

Fresh from a general overhaul at Inverurie Works, D30 no. 62430 *Jingling Geordie* had just arrived back at its home depot, Thornton Junction. A member of the shed staff checks the water levels. The names of the D30s were painted on the leading splasher.

23.8.55

Thornton Junction was one of the principal depots in the Scottish Region. Here D11/2 class no. 62671 *Bailie MacWheeble* of Eastfield shed, Glasgow, is being serviced. Alongside is D49 no. 62704 *Stirlingshire*, one of five members of the class allocated to Thornton. Over a hundred engines were on this depot's books in the mid-fifties.

23.8.55

Early evening with 3P no. 54471 turning at Elgin, a sub-shed of Keith depot, prior to working a passenger train back to its home depot, Inverness. The three types of 3P 4–4–0s were designed by three different Caledonian Railway Locomotive Superintendents in service. Examples of all three were to be found at Inverness.

24.8.55

During the mid-fifties you could still find examples of the ex-Great North of Scotland Railway D40 class 4–4–0s at work, although their days were numbered. No. 62271 at Keith had just completed its day's work, and the fire was being cleaned before coaling by the rather unusual crane arrangement on the right of the picture.

24.8.55

Fresh from a general overhaul at Inverurie Works, J35 class no. 64463 was in the process of working back to its home depot, Hawick. The engine was on shed at Dundee, where, having taken on coal and water, it was ready for the next stage of its journey back. Note the class and depot details painted on the buffer beam – this was normal practice in LNER days.

23.8.55

As with most of the other pre-Grouping railway companies the North British relied heavily on 0–6–0s. On the left is J37 no. 64608, a class introduced in 1911. No. 65329 is a J35, a class introduced by M. Holmes in 1888. The power classifications were 4F and 2F respectively. These two engines were photographed at Seafield.

22.8.55

Usually six of these J37 class 0–6–0s were to be found at Seafield. No. 64538 had recently undergone a general overhaul. Within a short time it would have been in the same work-stained condition as its surrounding classmates.

22.8.55

Another of the J37s, no. 64636, in trouble at Polmont. It has lost its front wheels. The crane standing nearby had presumably been used to lift the locomotive. The tender had also been uncoupled while work was in progress.

22.8.55

At least two J37 class locomotives were under repair at Polmont at the time of my visit. No. 64571 was minus its coupling rods, and numerous parts were lying around. Repairs were usually carried out at the northern end of the depot. The J37s were built to the design of W.P. Reid for the North British Railway and introduced in 1914.

22.8.55

J35 class engines were a common sight at Aberdeen Kittybrewster. No. 64529 was a Bathgate engine that had visited Inverurie Works and was in the process of working back to its home depot. There were two sheds at Aberdeen. Kittybrewster was of Great North of Scotland Railway origin, while Ferryhill was shared by the Caledonian Railway and the North British Railway in pre-Grouping days.

24.8.55

The vacuum-assisted turntable at Aberdeen Kittybrewster made life much easier for enginemen. Here J35 n. 64482 is being turned. This was an ex-Great North of Scotland Railway depot of half-roundhouse type.

24.8.55

With the massive coaling plant at Aberdeen Kittybrewster shed in the background, J35 class no. 64482 awaits its next turn of duty. Note the 'No. 6' painted on the tender – presumably this referred to the work allocated to the engine.

24.8.55

The driver of ex-Caledonian Railway 3F 0–6–0 no. 57597 prepares the engine at Keith to work back to its home depot, Inverness. The B1 no. 61347 was allocated to Aberdeen Kittybrewster depot.

24.8.55

The thirty-five examples of the J38 class introduced by Sir Nigel Gresley in 1926 were all allocated to depots in Scotland. They were classified 6F, having a higher tractive effort than the much more numerous and similar-looking J39s which were rated 4F. No. 65910 had run into trouble with a hot box on the middle set of driving wheels and is pictured outside the repair shop at Thornton Junction.

23.8.55

C15 class no. 67463 was nearing the end of its working life when this picture was taken. It was withdrawn the following month. Four of these 4–4–2Ts designed by W.P. Reid for the North British Railway and introduced in 1911 were allocated to Polmont in the early fifties. Note the small hand-operated crane on the right.

22.8.55

Shining like a new pin, this is N15 class no. 69152
at St Margaret's, fresh from a general overhaul.
No doubt it wouldn't take long to build up a
coating of grime! The N15s were a fairly large class
with ninety-nine examples in service at the time.

21.8.55

The C16 class 4–4–2Ts were designed by W.P. Reid for the North British Railway and introduced in 1915, four years after the C15 class. No. 67493, seen here at Thornton, was a Dundee engine. Ten of the twenty-one members of the class were allocated there.

23.8.55

Dundee Tay Bridge depot was home to over ninety locomotives in the mid-fifties. Here two of its allocation await their next duties. On the left is J35 class no. 64631, alongside J83 class no. 68452. Originally a North British Railway depot, it was to become one of the last steam sheds in Scotland, retaining its steam allocation until May 1967.

23.8.55

J83 class no. 68465 busy on shunting work at Dundee. Introduced in 1900 to the design of M. Holmes, the J83s were to be found at many Scottish depots. No. 68465 was withdrawn in August 1957; after a short period in store it was cut up at Kilmarnock Works in October 1957.

23.8.55

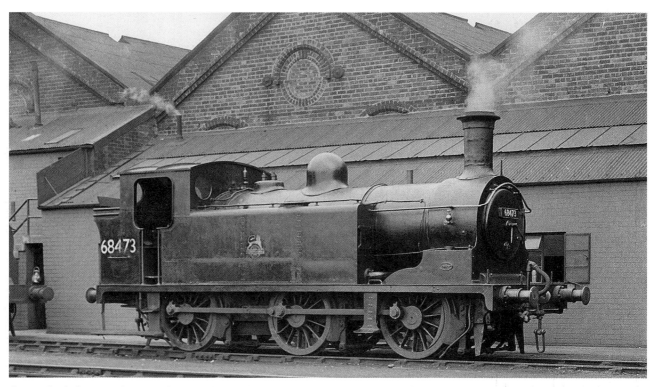

Several of the J83 class in the Edinburgh area were principally used as carriage pilots. No. 68473, seen here at Haymarket depot, was in good external condition and had almost certainly received a general overhaul not long before this picture was taken.

22.8.55

Dundee had just one of these ex-Great Eastern Railway J69/1s in its allocation, no. 68551, fitted with a rather unsightly stovepipe chimney. There were a very small number of this class to be found in Scotland in the mid-fifties, together with a single F4 2–4–2T at Kittybrewster.

23.8.55

The Aberdeen area was still served by several locomotives that originated from pre-Grouping railway companies south of the border. F4 2–4–2T was of Great Eastern origin while N2 0–6–2T was a Great North Railway design. J72 class 0–6–0T no. 68710, seen here at Aberdeen Kittybrewster depot, was a North Eastern Railway design.

24.8.55

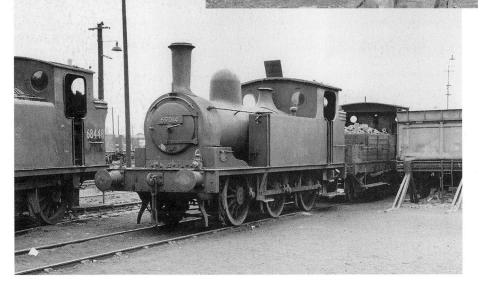

During the fifties you could find various representatives of North Eastern and Great Eastern Railway designs working in Scotland. J72 class no. 69014 was the youngest of the locomotives to be found at South Leith. The J72s were a design first introduced in 1898 by W. Worsdell for the North Eastern. This example was one of the batch built after nationalisation.

21.8.55

On Sunday mornings most of South Leith's shunters could be found resting. J88 no. 68342 and Y9 no. 68104 were both North British Railway designs. W.P. Reid introduced the J88s with their distinctive tall chimneys in 1904. The Y9s were older, making their debut in 1882 to the design of M. Holmes. Note that both types have solid buffers.

21.8.55

Only one of the four ex-Great North of Scotland 0–4–2Ts, no. 68191, was at work at the time of my visit. Here Z4 no. 68190 and Z5 no. 68192 await an increase in dock traffic at Aberdeen Kittybrewster. Both were in good external condition and unlike no. 68193 carried the BR emblem.

24.8.55

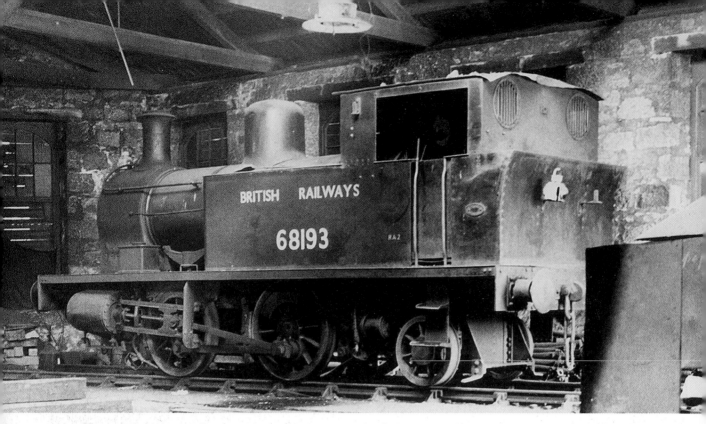

I was particularly keen to photograph the ex-Great North of Scotland 0–4–2Ts of classes Z4 and Z5, both Manning Wardle designs built for the railway in 1915. The two Z4s had 3ft 6in driving wheels and 13 × 20in outside cylinders, while the two Z5s had 4ft driving wheels and 14 × 20in outside cylinders. No. 68193, still lettered British Railways, had not worked for some time and was tucked away in a rather inaccessible corner at Aberdeen Kittybrewster depot.

24.8.55

The Dundee shed pilot Y9 class no. 68100, complete with spark arrestor and wooden tender. Six Y9s were allocated to the shed at this time and were used as shed pilots and for shunting where tight curves existed.

23.8.55

The wooden tenders fitted to the Y9 class were of various shapes and sizes. The largest concentration of the class was to be found in the Edinburgh area. Their principal duties were shunting at Leith docks and at several other locations. No. 68115, seen here at South Leith, was built in 1897 and withdrawn in July 1957.

21.8.55

The Caledonian Railway 'Pugs' were fitted with large conventional buffers in contrast to the solid forms fitted to the North British Railway Y9s. No. 56035 was a stranger in the camp at St Margaret's. Like the Y9s, the 'Pugs' ran with a four-wheeled wooden tender.

21.8.55

Y9 no. 68099, complete with wooden tender, at the tank roundhouse at St Margaret's. This locomotive was built at Cowlairs in 1889 and notched up sixty-seven years' service. Thirty-five members of the class were built, and thirty-three made it into British Railways stock although three were withdrawn before receiving their BR numbers.

21.8.55

Only one example of the Y9 class has survived into preservation, no. 68095, seen here in its working days at Seafield, a sub-shed of St Margaret's. The engine was still lettered British Railways and was running with the familiar wooden tender. This engine was built at Cowlairs in 1887.

22.8.55